INDUSTRIAL RELATIONS

T0345979

INDUSTRIAL RELATIONS

INAUGURAL LECTURE

by

JOHN HILTON, M.A.

MONTAGUE BURTON PROFESSOR OF
INDUSTRIAL RELATIONS IN THE
UNIVERSITY OF CAMBRIDGE

CAMBRIDGE

AT THE UNIVERSITY PRESS

1931

CAMBRIDGE
UNIVERSITY PRESS

University Printing House, Cambridge CB2 8BS, United Kingdom

Published in the United States of America by Cambridge University Press, New York

Cambridge University Press is part of the University of Cambridge.

It furthers the University's mission by disseminating knowledge in the pursuit of education, learning and research at the highest international levels of excellence.

www.cambridge.org
Information on this title: www.cambridge.org/9781107650213

© Cambridge University Press 1931

First published 1931
Re-issued 2014

A catalogue record for this publication is available from the British Library

ISBN 978-1-107-65021-3 Paperback

INDUSTRIAL RELATIONS

THE MONTAGUE BURTON CHAIR of Industrial Relations, of which I have the honour to be the first occupant, is charged with the study of the conditions of employment and the relations between employers and employed, with special reference to the causes of industrial disputes and the methods of promoting industrial peace.

At the moment the matters for the study of which the Chair was founded are not in the forefront of public concern. There is peace in industry, if by peace one means an absence of open conflict. At the moment the relations of employers and employed are not causing anxiety; the anxiety is on the part of the employers and the employed. To-day the conditions of employment are not a pressing concern; masters and men alike are more concerned with the condition of unemployment.

This uneasy peace, mutual anxiety, and re-direction of concern, is not born of industrial causes: it is the result of forces that have broken in upon industry from without.

For the present, therefore, the occupant of the Chair of Industrial Relations must, whether he likes it or not, whether it is strictly within his province or not, find himself preoccupied with the state of industry; the abject state of industry as the victim of external forces.

Industry itself can generate quite enough waste, friction, race, slip and breakdown to satisfy any moderate-minded mocker at Western industrial civilisation. But, with all its blundering and confusion, industry gets on with its job. It may muddle along, but it muddles ahead. There are brains, energy, creative vision, organisation and purpose, of a sort, in industry. Given anything like the same qualities and behaviour on the part of other sections of the body politic, national and international, industry can and will deliver the goods.

Here are employers with ever improving technique, processes, apparatus, organisation, products; still very far, no doubt, from 100 per cent. perfection, but always perfecting, even through the catastrophic last few years. Here are workpeople ready and able to throw energy, intelligence, skill into their part of the industrial alliance. They may at times and in places have queer notions of what is right and what is wrong, of what is good and what is bad, in industrial matters: their will to do a fair day's work for a fair day's pay may sometimes flag: but they can and do work (when they are allowed) and they work well.

These two partners in industry are in a world which has a limitless though erratic appetite for the products of their joint activities. There has been no set-back in the machinery whereby the things that are made are taken from those who make them and put into the hands of those who want them: on the contrary a constant improvement in the means of transport, advertisement, and sale. Industry has done its job, and wants only to go on with its job.

There it is, the whole industrial system— and it is all in a state of paralysis. For years past it has been under a spell: its limbs stiffened, its sinews held, by forces so uncanny that in an earlier age men would have smelt witchcraft. What power could doom these employers, despite all efforts, to go from loss to loss; what power could put two and three-quarter million people on the streets who want to earn their bread by useful labour; what power could deny them even the goods they themselves are prepared to make? What else, if not witchcraft?

Nowadays belief in witchcraft is out of fashion. We look for natural causes of unnatural occurrences. Yet we do still turn a suspicious eye towards the one thing in our earthly midst that still retains something of the occult. We are not at all sure about Finance. It seems to have powers not very different from the Evil Eye. Perhaps, after all, it is the same thing. Finance—witchcraft, witchcraft—finance.

The Chair from which I derive the grace to speak to-night is a Chair of Industrial Relations and even the weaving of spells by magicians I will approach from that base, keeping touch on industrial wood.

Industrial Relations have their scriptures. They are known as 'Collective Agreements between Employers and Workpeople'. There are said to be at least eight thousand such documents operative at this moment. They regulate, by voluntary mutual agreement, the working lives of many millions of our workpeople: the wages they shall receive, the hours they shall work, the people they shall work with, the conditions of their employment. They are the industrial code. They enshrine the letter, and much of the spirit, of Industrial Relations.

The witch-doctor casts his spell over industrial agreements. A wand is waved and their blessings are turned to curses. The spell works on, and industrial agreements at the next change of the moon turn into industrial disagreements.

The method of the black magic is fatally simple: it merely alters a value; only one value among many, but the transmogrification of this one bedevils the rest.

Industrial agreements presuppose stable values. If colliers agree to hew coal for so much a ton, they expect a ton to remain a ton; and it does. If weavers agree to weave at so much a yard, they depend on a yard to remain a yard; and it does. If turners agree to work a 47 hour week, they depend on an hour to remain an hour; and it does. These units are stable. The black art cannot touch them.

But what of the other unit? The crux of most agreements is in a figure which says that the pay shall be so many shillings. If the collier, the weaver, the fitter agree that the pay shall be so many shillings, they hope that a shilling will remain a shilling. It does not. An incantation is uttered over a financial cauldron, and the shilling, in seven days and seven nights, is worth now ninepence, now fourpence, now half-a-crown. So, in turn, employers and workers must denounce their agreements. They are torn across. The fragments are thrown into the cauldron. There is a blue flame, a sulphurous smell, and a new trouble is brewed. The witch-doctor shows no glee; he has had no idea either what he was doing or what he has done. He is interested in his spells, not in what they spell.

The shilling does not remain a shilling; and the wage-earners and wage-payers who have made a bargain they would stand by, cannot keep that bargain because unseen powers tamper with its terms. Prices fall, and the employer finds himself paying more in wages cost than he reckoned for; prices rise, and the worker finds himself with less beef and bread and beer and boots than he bargained for. Both have been taught that the shilling is a medium of exchange. They find it much like some other mediums. Its phenomena are not always genuine.

If this were all, a talisman might be found.

All collective agreements might have a clause providing that the money to be paid should vary with the cost of living. Some two million wage- and salary-earners already work under such agreements. The idea is that whatever happens to the value of the shilling the wage-man shall get the same amount of meal and malt and gear for a week's work that he bargained for when his agreement was signed. An excellent idea. A charm to ward off spells. Distribute the charm to all wage- and salary-earners and all will be immune.

In industry, as in life, the cleverest and most ingenious schemes are not always the most liked. Even among the two millions there are grumblers. They complain that one cost-of-living index-number does not fit all persons. That is true. But a thousand index-numbers would not suit all persons, for no two persons are alike. Ten index-numbers for ten broad groups might be better than one: but who is to compile them, and who is to say which man belongs to which group? If the principle be accepted, one index-number is good enough to ensure rough justice. Nor do the employers of the two millions all rejoice in the scheme. It is an anxious thing to tender for an order in money when you do not know what your money wage-bill will be; and when wages jump about with percentage changes in the cost of living it complicates the pay-sheets. So you fix up a scheme whereby the adjustment is not made too often in the year. In the Civil Service the change is made once every six months, at the end of March and the end of September, with the untoward result that the civil servant gets higher wages in the summer when prices are low, and lower wages in the winter when prices are high.

Because the change is made infrequently, when it comes it comes with a jump. Now the change of prices is a day-to-day affair. The housewife adjusts herself to it. When the cost-of-living bonus changes it is a sudden drop or rise. No one objects to the sudden rise; but no one likes the sudden drop. It is felt. It hurts. This makes a cost-of-living sliding scale a poor substitute to the wage-earner for a stable shilling. Still, it is a good second best; and if the worker were the only sufferer from the witch-dance of the shilling, one could tinker up the talisman to make it work more quickly and more surely.

Even in recent months great minds have dallied with the notion that the reluctance of

wages in general to fall with the fall in prices
was the one and only cause, or at any rate
the major cause, of most of our industrial
woes. As recently as June last Sir Josiah
Stamp popularised, in the columns of *The
Times*, the thesis first propounded by Dr
Rueff, the able and distinguished French
economist, that unemployment, and by in-
ference industrial stagnation, was directly
related to, and probably attributable to, the
keeping up of wages while prices fell.

On this question I speak with a due sense
of the responsibility that attaches to the oc-
cupancy of the Chair of Industrial Relations
at Cambridge University. It is a jealously
guarded tradition of the great universities
that those who speak from their Chairs may
utter their personal views without fear, without prior approval, without subsequent re-
proach; for that their expressed opinions
neither commit nor implicate anyone but
themselves. To one who has been for a dozen
years a reasonably well-behaved civil servant,
emergence into such freedom is a little
dazzling. But, here as elsewhere, self-re-
straint grows as restraint is removed. What
I have to say will be said under the discipline
of knowing that I know very little and that

what I believe I know may turn out to be wrong.

The argument, first enunciated by Dr Rueff in 1925, is that the immediate cause of unemployment in Great Britain is the failure of wages to adapt themselves to the level of prices. The proof adduced is that an examination of the figures discloses a permanent relation between the movement of numbers unemployed and the movement of the level of real wages. The reason given for the faulty adaptation of wages to prices is the power and discipline of British trade unions, which offer stubborn resistance to the reduction of wages, and the British policy of paying unemployment benefit, which bolsters up a wage level that would otherwise rightly fall. The conclusion drawn is that only if prices rise without wages rising, or if wages fall without prices falling, only then will unemployment in Great Britain return to its pre-war level.

The basic facts may be taken as agreed. Weekly rates of wages, reckoned in money, are probably about 70 per cent. higher than they were just before the war. But the working week is shorter, and, if we make full allowance for that, hourly rates of wages are probably about 90 per cent. higher than they were in the spring of 1914. That is the gain to the wage-earner in money; it must be offset by the increase in the prices of the things he buys. The cost of living is computed to be 46 per cent. higher than before the war. Allowing for that, it appears that the average wage-receiver is to-day better off in 'real wages' (that is the purchasing power of the money he receives) as compared with just before the war, by something like 17 per cent. in weekly wages or 32 per cent. in hourly wages. That is a substantial improvement in the standard of living of the wage-earner who is in work. Its actuality will be borne out by anyone with a knowledge of working-class conditions at the two periods.

'Before the war' is now a long time ago. It was by no means a golden age from which we may confidently measure our progress or our backslidings. Moreover, much has happened since then. The sooner we stop referring to it as a standard of comparison the better. So take 1924, which was a moderately good year, as we reckon good years nowadays. Since then the cost of living has fallen, but the money wages of those in full work have remained much the same, with the result that the wages of the wage-receiver are now worth roughly 20 per cent. more in buying power than in November 1924.

These are the agreed, or not seriously disputed, facts. Back now to the argument, that the increased real wages have caused the increased unemployment: and first to its statistical proof. It is shown that if you divide the index of wages by the index of prices, you get a series of 'real wage' figures which, if drawn out in a diagram, give a curve which looks very much like the curve of unemployment. As real wages go up, unemployment goes up, as 'real wages' come down, unemployment comes down.

Mark this, however. To get this tell-tale curve one must divide wages, not by the cost of living, but by wholesale prices. What precisely the ratios yielded by that operation are supposed to represent I do not know. They are certainly not indices of real wages, for real wages depend on the cost of living. They are certainly not indices of the employer's wage-cost relative to the market price of his products, for the wholesale price index includes imported goods and neither is, nor ever was intended to be, an index of the price the employer gets for his goods. It is certainly not a measure of changes in the proportion of the national income that goes in wages, for the national income does not move in accordance with the wholesale price index. I cannot even guess what it might be argued to represent. I think it is a tale of ratios and correlations—signifying nothing.

It is true that if one divides the wages index by the wholesale prices index the curve one gets, viewed from a distance with half-closed eyes, looks something like the unemployment curve. It is true that if one suitably magnifies the scale of the meaningless curve it can be made to look as though it had the same amplitude as the other. From this the unwary will proceed to draw weighty conclusions. The wary will look a little closer, and observe that for many years the wages index has hardly moved. Since 1924 it has moved only 2 per cent. and that by almost imperceptible stages. In this curious operation of dividing wages by wholesale prices the wholesale prices are being divided into an almost unchanging quantity. That being so, the mysterious curve that has been obtained is no other than the inverse of the prices curve. It is the wholesale prices curve turned upside-down.

You may take the indices of any series of

data which change little from year to year, divide them by the wholesale price indices, and get a similar curve. If this be proof of the cause of unemployment, astonishing results can be got from its wider application. One may divide wholesale prices into the average height of the population, or the mean annual temperature at Cambridge, make a curve of the results, put it alongside the unemployment curve, and prove incontestably that unemployment is entirely due to people stubbornly remaining too tall, or to the perverse refusal of the mean annual temperature at Cambridge to fall in sympathy with the fall in wholesale prices.

You will see now why it is necessary for the purposes of this argument to divide wages by wholesale prices, and not by the cost of living. If you invert the cost of living curve it does not give you what even looks like second cousin to the unemployment curve. But if you invert the wholesale prices curve you get a quite noticeable family resemblance. Of course you do. But there is nothing new in that. It is true, and it is tremendously important; but it is not new, and it has nothing to do, at first rebound, with wages. The correlations that struck Dr Rueff and impressed Sir Josiah Stamp are not correlations between wages and unemployment, but between wholesale prices and unemployment. It is true and vastly important that when the general level of prices is falling unemployment increases and that when the level of prices is rising unemployment declines. That is all the unnameable curve has proved. It is the increasing-unemployment story of the last ten years. It is in part the decreasing-unemployment story of the last nine weeks. It is the unemployment story of the last two years, not only for this country, but for every industrial country in the world. Wages certainly come into the story, but they come in at the end, not at the beginning; and they come in, as you shall hear, rather more as the hero than the villain. We may be dubious about some aspects of the character and conduct of Jack the Giant Killer; but we must give him credit for killing the giant.

So here we are back at our witchcraft. Not only does the conjuration of monetary values bewitch the collective agreements of employers and workpeople, it weaves a spell over industry itself; it draws the furnaces, puts grit in the bearings, knocks off the belts, and puts two million or more men and women on the streets, on the dole. It widens the magic circle—not with intent, for it has no discoverable intent—and the industry of the world is spell-bound. Twenty million, forty million men and women in every part of the habitable globe are without work, hungry, and desperate.

Spell-bound, and slightly ridiculous. Many a writer of ancient lore has told how, when the wizard had cast his spell on the young prince, fastened his hands behind him, and made him walk backward when he wanted to go forward, how the rude unmannerly scion of a distant house had not been able to forbear laughing in his face. I hope the Russians, a polite and good-natured people, are restraining themselves. They will need their breath, anyhow, to cool their porridge.

But ours is a mechanical age; our similes should be more suited to our times: so let me couple enchantment with mechanism and say that employers and employed have appeared, for these many years, as people trying to carry on their job and maintain their good relations in a financial vehicle which has been careering down hill with controls that don't work, with brakes that alternately jam and slip, with an unaccountable steering gear, and with a driver neither drunk nor incapable, merely bewitched.

Nine weeks ago we jumped clear of the international tumbril. It was a nasty fall, but we were soon on our feet, with no more than a few bruises. Prices are rising, and, that being so, workpeople are going back to work. Employers will make profits where before they made losses. We could jump because we were not, just then, carrying much weight. Our jump and the jump of those who followed us has lightened the load and improved a little the control of the crazy thing that was carrying us all nearer the precipice: but the fright has not gone out of the eyes of those who are left. Perhaps others yet will jump; but gold is a heavy metal, and those whose pockets are too full may find their movements impeded.

The contention that post-war unemployment, and in particular the additional unemployment of the last two years, has been due to the failure of wages to fall with the fall of prices, I reject outright. I go further and say that if wages the world over had been tied to prices, the fall in wages would have contributed to a still further and steeper fall in prices and there would have been more, not less, unemployment than there is to-day. The effect would have been that of tying a tin can to a dog's tail.

We sometimes find, after the event, that we have cause to be thankful for some sheer mule-headedness that infuriated us at the time. Let us now thank our stars that organised labour, with more acquiescence from organised capital than is generally supposed, stuck its feet mulishly in the slippery mud. It slid a little, but not much. The position was plain to see had we had eyes to see it: if wages stood firm and refused to follow prices, prices would have to come back to wages. It is happening. I pay here my belated respects to one who died three weeks ago, one who gave his life for his cause, if ever man did. A. J. Cook, the Miners' Secretary, muddle-headed, staunch-hearted, had the sense that is deeper than knowledge. 'Not a minute on the day, not a penny off the pay.' He refused to budge, whoever else might waver, until he was beaten helpless. It was not in him to reason his case, but his intuitions were true. They told him he was right and he was right. He had a great soul. May it go marching on.

The immediate cause of the industrial

paralysis and of the increasing unemployment of the last two years has been, not anything arising within industry, not any failure of matters adjustable by industrial relations, but the fall in the price level. If you think to put industry in its place by asking it what is the cause of the changes in the purchasing power of money, and what it suggests should be done to keep the price level steady, I answer that you must send that question to the right address. Industry is not in the magic business; it is not expert in the black arts. They are not its job. If you then say it has no right to criticise I answer that it claims as much right to criticise finance as the non-industrialist would rightly claim to criticise industry, if industry were to make the same sad mess of its job. If the motor-car made by industry were as erratic and undependable an affair as the price level made by finance, if it wobbled and blundered about the roads of the world, landing its passengers where they never wanted to go, hurling them out at every other street corner, crashing into shops and factories and scattering their goods to be spoiled or picked up by the wrong people, the least expert onlooker would be entitled to say, and would say, 'That is not a good motor-car,

I think it must be a bad machine running on a bad spirit. I think that owners and designers and managers ought to be ashamed of themselves'.

The view I have taken about wages, if sound, has important implications for the immediate future. I must now lay stress upon the distinction between the *movement* of wages, prices and unemployment, and the *levels* of wages, prices and unemployment when stability is reached, when the magicians have blundered upon and are engrossed in the weaving of other spells which do not bewitch the price level. It is the movement of the price level that has been the immediate cause of the increase in unemployment; it is movement of the price level that will draw the unemployed back to work. I say 'will draw' because the increased activity and the reduction in unemployment that has taken place in the last nine weeks is immediately due not so much to a movement in the price level as to the suction upon British goods set up by the partial vacuum of exchange differentials. That is a temporary advantage: it will serve its good turn, and come to an end. The rise in home prices which will accompany that process will also serve its turn, and come to an end. What is taking place so far is not in-flation: let us call it un-deflation. If 1924 be taken as an empiric normality, we can healthily un-deflate some 40 points in whole-sale prices, some 17 points in the cost of living, and some 2 points in money wages. That would bring us back, in each case, to the 100 mark of 1924. That would be no more than the restoring of the anaemic patient to such normal health as he more or less enjoyed in 1924.

You will have realised already what this programme implies: a deflation of real wages of round about 15 per cent. If something of that kind has not happened when we have got back to our 1924 price level and settled down there, we may be left with our old accustomed figure of a million and a quarter unemployed, and perhaps more.

For we are considering now, not move-ment, but levels. We are considering what the *position* is after the movement has taken place. This is quite another story from the story that unemployment was caused by the failure of wages to *move* as prices moved.

Prominence was first given to the analytical method I now adopt by Sir Henry Strakosch in a special supplement of *The Economist* issued in July 1930. To illustrate his argument he adopted an informed guess that of the estimated total national income of £4000 millions in 1924 about half went in wages and salaries, about one-quarter in receipts of interest on fixed-interest-bearing securities, some odd amounts on other kinds of receipts, and about 17 per cent. went in the form of profits to investors in industrial enterprises. He argued, very cogently as it seems to me, that if the wage-earner and the rentier had their share of the whole increased by reason of an increase in real wages and real interest following automatically upon a fall in prices, someone must lose to an equivalent extent; and the only class from whom the amount could be taken away was the class deriving its income from the profits of enterprise. It would follow that when this process is complete industry must be less profitable, the investment of savings in industrial enterprise must decline; and workpeople whose continued employment is causing a loss must be discharged. That is the static, as distinct from the dynamic, argument for high unemployment being an accompaniment, when stability is reached, of unduly high real wages.

The *increase* of unemployment has been due,

not to the increase in real wages, but to the fall in prices. Let me keep a firm hold on that. The present argument is that an unduly high *level* of real wages, when stability is reached, may leave a stagnant pool of unemployment. The two propositions are not mutually exclusive: indeed, I think they are simultaneously tenable.

The cost of living has fallen, wages have held, real wages and real interest have both had an unearned, unasked, increment. The witch-doctors certainly never intended that, but they never intended anything, for they have been engrossed in witchcraft, not statecraft. I think it is true that real wages and real interest in Great Britain are to-day higher than industry can bear. We could not, as an economic community, stabilise healthily at that apportionment of the national income. Industry would have to live on its fat, which is already very lean. No one would feed it with the capital that comes from savings. Existing enterprises would languish. It would be better to shut down than to invite capital into a concern on a prospectus that was false in a material particular, the particular being that costs were higher than earnings. That spells contraction and unemployment.

So, as prices rise, real wages and real interest must lose their unearned increment. The average level of wage-rates stood almost firm while prices fell, and perhaps thereby saved economic civilisation from disaster; wages must stand equally firm while prices rise and allow economic recovery.

The employers of the two millions who are on cost of living sliding scales and whose wages have fallen with the fall in retail prices will, I hope, abide by their agreements. These workers, having gained nothing by the fall, will lose nothing by the rise. Those others, the miners, the steel workers, the shipwrights, and the engineers, who, though not on sliding scales, have suffered heavy reductions in wages owing to the exposed nature of their industries, will, I hope, secure increases greater than the increases in the cost of living. But if that large intermediate group of wage-earners, most of them in the sheltered or quasi-monopolistic industries, whose wage-rates have been maintained throughout the recent catastrophic fall in prices, use their organised strength to keep the advantages they have automatically and unexpectedly gained by the fall in the cost of living, the share of wages in the national income will still be out of balance, industries will still run at a loss, savings will not be invested in genuine enterprise, our overseas trade will decline, and unemployment will continue.

As with the wage-earner, so with the salary-earner and the receiver of interest. What is good for the goose is good for the gander. The bond-holder, the recipient of fixed sums of money, whether in the form of debenture dividends, interest on State or municipal loans, rents, interest on mortgages, fixed salaries or what not, has profited, equally with the wage-earner, by the fall in prices: an unasked, un-earned, increment. One reason for the re-luctance to enforce a policy of wage-reduction has been the difficulty of enforcing an equi-valent fall in real interest. Who with a sense of equity could ask the wage-earner to forgo his gains while the interest-receiver kept his? Now the rentier and the landlord and the pro-fessor, along with the wage-earner, must lose the supplement that was thrust into his hands.

Just as the gain to the wage-earners and the rentier was not so great as might appear; so the loss will have its compensations. To the wage-earner the decline in the real wages of those at work, if accompanied by an increase in the numbers at work and by an assurance of the greater regularity of work, will go far to make up the reduction in the real value of rates per hour. To the recipient of fixed income the reduction in taxation which should in due course follow the reduction in the heavy drain upon public funds occasioned by a reduction of the numbers unemployed, coupled with the improved yield to the Exchequer which should follow upon an improvement in trade activity and a restored level of prices, will moderate somewhat the amount he will have to forgo.

For the burden of unemployment benefit has been heavy upon the worker, upon the employer, upon the taxpayer. It has been evident for many years past that the Unemployment Insurance Scheme called for a thorough-going reconsideration. I do not mean the removal of anomalies, the checking of abuses, the adjustment of benefit rates. That could be done at any time, has been continuously done, is being done now. I mean, not that, but a reconsideration of the part to be played by Unemployment Insurance as a permanent feature of our economic, social and political order. 'Insurance' is a misnomer for a compulsory scheme which undertakes to compensate against incalculable risks. Contributions to the unemployment fund are not insurance premiums, they are taxes levied at a flat rate upon workers as a class, and upon employers as a class, with assistance from the taxpayers who include both workers and employers, to alleviate the distress caused by irrational disasters whose magnitude, time and continuance cannot, in our economic abjectness, be foretold. If the sea were subject to wizardry, and could be lashed into tempests enduring two, five, ten years, to talk of 'insurance' of shipping would be mere idle chatter.

In a world not afflicted with what we so accurately call 'spells' of unemployment (it is curious how words reveal subconscious interpretations), in such a world there would be a rightful place for real unemployment insurance. Whether the function of insuring against such unemployment is a function proper to the State or more proper to industry is still an open question. The statesman holds an incorrectible conviction that the State can actively intervene in one province of economic territory and leave the rest unaffected. He will take charge of unemployment. He will receive and maintain the persons whom industry cannot use: but he will draw the line there, and go no further. He will take them as they come, he avows that he will not regulate their coming. But he finds, inevitably, that his intervention in the part affects the whole. It may be that the State will have to choose between freeing itself of the responsibility for unemployment relief, and accepting responsibility, not only for the unemployed but for the conduct of industry.

In saying this, I would not be held to subscribe to the view that the British Unemployment Insurance Scheme has bolstered up the wage-level, and thereby caused unemployment. The contention that 'the dole' has stiffened the resistance of organised labour against wage-reductions is a contention that is incapable of either proof or disproof. The argument is based on the supposition that we are still living in an individualistic world of free competition. It pictures an unemployed man, on the brink of starvation, helpless, hopeless and desperate, going to an employer and saying 'I must have work and wages. The rate you are paying is 50s. a week. Give me 48s. and I will work for you', whereupon the employer, glad of the cheaper labour, takes him on, and dismisses one of his 50s. men, who in turn stays unemployed until he can hold out no longer, and in turn offers his services for 48*s*. a week. A beautiful picture of delicate adjustments. It has only one flaw, that nothing like it happens in the actual world in which we live. In that world individualistic free competition has been elbowed out by collective organisation. Trade unions and employers' organisations existed before 'the dole' was born, or even thought of. They, and not the marginal unit, determine what the level of wages shall be. Wages are not determined by any nibbling at the edges, but by the impact of unified masses. One can theorise that the effect of unemployment benefit has been to make the lowest-paid workman refuse to accept wages near the level of his unemployment pay; one can establish an equally strong case that the payment of unemployment benefit to the docker and the textile operative has acted as a subsidy to wages and enabled the employer to pay lower wages. The one case is as good as the other. This also one can definitely say, that the fact of unemployment benefit has not been a discoverable factor in any important wage negotiations that have taken place in the last two years. No employers have said to themselves 'If it were not for the dole we could discharge these stubborn fellows and easily get others at lower wages'. Employers neither talk nor think such nonsense. No trade union has winked the other eye, saying 'that dole means no more blacklegs'. Indeed, they have said almost the exact opposite. I suspect this theory to be based on a muddled notion that a body of workpeople can down tools, walk into an Employment Exchange, and demand the dole. They cannot. Benefit is not paid to people on strike.

I said that if prices rise to the 1924 level, the restoration of economic health requires that real wages shall fall to the 1924 level. Let me now add an important qualification. If, as the result of joint effort on the part of employers and workpeople, production per head of workers employed is greater to-day than in 1924, then labour is entitled to its share of extra product and its real wages can be increased without loss to any other group; indeed, leaving a due measure of gain to all others. Most of these arguments about real wages suppose that output per head has remained constant. It has not: it has increased. The statistics are not good enough to enable one to say by how much; but it has increased greatly as compared with 1914, and it has certainly continued to increase since 1924. Let no one try to tell labour that it must work with capital to produce more, but be content with the same slice out of the larger cake. That tale won't go down.

It is to the credit of capital and labour that output per unit of labour (and probably of capital too) has increased even in recent years. No one can put much heart into increased production when one worker in five is already unemployed and every new improvement in plant and method seems to throw still more out on the streets. Perhaps improving trade will remove this obstacle. Yet there is another side to the picture. I have heard employers say in desperation, of men on piecework, 'the only way to get these fellows to stick to their work is to lower their wages. They have a certain standard of living. When they have earned enough for that they just knock off': and I knew, in the particular cases, it was true. Adversity stings both masters and men to hard work; prosperity makes for easy going. I blame no man for preferring an easy life on modest means to riches won by sweat and weariness. Odd people here and there can have both ease and riches; but people in the mass cannot. If labour claims high real wages it must give high productivity. That is the one safe and certain base.

'But', says labour, 'how do we know that we are getting, or will get our fair share. What is the formula?' There is no formula which will determine what wages in this or that industry, at one time and another, are just about right. It is a triangular contest between the worker, the investor, and the public for who shall increase or safeguard his slice of the product; with the entrepreneur doing his best to harmonise the conflicting claims, and the speculator bobbing in and out, upsetting everyone's calculations. No formula; but a code, that each contestant shall observe the rules of the ring. One rule is that there shall be honest disclosure of the facts; another is that the contest for slices of the thing that is made shall not stop the making of it; and another is that if you consent to a referee you abide by his verdict.

It is sometimes better to fight than to reason; but it is generally better to reason than to fight.

There is excellent machinery for the reasoned consideration of conflicting claims in many industries. Where it aids enlightenment, reasoning, and good temper a conciliator can be brought in from outside. Where a deadlock has been reached an arbitrator can be appointed. The most successful conciliator is the one who makes each side see the other side's case; the most successful arbitrator is the one who guesses the mid-point between what each side thinks it would get as the settlement at the end of a prolonged strike. The good arbitrator gets the result without the strike.

There is, of course, the Soviet system, under which all goods are made for the community, commandeered on behalf of the community, and distributed on some combination of economic and doctrinal principles, by a hierarchy of committees, under the eye of the Party, to the reinforcement of capital or the maintenance of labour. The British worker would not enjoy the Soviet system, and, unless driven to it in desperation by some more than usually fantastic bedevilment conjured up by the magicians, he will not go in for it. But let the wizards take care; they have blundered Europe to the brink of Sovietism, and if they do not better learn to control their magic, it will go. With what we see of capitalist economy before our eyes, and with what we can foresee of the consequences of further bungling, there is a lot to be said for Sovietism; and it will be said, and will be listened to. Either that or we shall relapse from industrialism. One recourse the city-dwelling Israelite had in reserve against the follies and tyrannies of rulers was 'Back to your tents, O Israel'. If finance cannot do its job we may have to choose between Moscow and the desert.

I speak, you will observe, of Finance, not of financiers; just as it is our habit to speak of Industry, not industrialists. The indictment industry makes against finance, is not an indictment of persons, but of functions embodied in an apparatus which embraces capital, currency and credit, and which embodies not only the activities of bankers, financiers, brokers and jobbers, but also those of State Treasuries on the one hand and of the investor and the speculator-gambler on the other. It is the whole complex that has let industry down. One personifies, quite rightly I think, this complex of functions and attributes. One expects, and properly expects, not financiers, not bankers, not one man or ten men, but Finance to have a corporate intelligence, purpose, and programme; a corporate sense and a corporate spirit.

Industry can and will find employment, pay wages, adjust its differences, deliver the goods. It only asks that the purchasing power of its customers shall be allowed to expand in accordance with the expansion of productive power, that the value of money shall remain reasonably constant, and that savings shall be permitted to flow into creative enterprise. These three things are the job of Finance. Let Finance, first, realise and admit that it has a job, and, second, do it.

'But', you may say, neatly returning my service, 'Finance *is* magic. The control of Finance *is* witchcraft. Industry can make a motor-car, and can be held to account if it works badly; for a motor-car is a mere earthly thing. Finance is essentially an un-earthly thing. It cannot be held to account because it is unaccountable. No magician can foretell what his magic will conjure up. He is liable to be as much startled as anyone when the spell that should have merely made the cauldron burn with a golden flame turns the pig blue instead'.

I agree. Then one of two things; either let us have an authoritative science of witch-craft, or let us ponder whether black magic is not a debased survival of a once clean faith to which Finance must return, or we perish.

It is not a mere chance that 'I believe' has been spilt into creed and into credit; that the only Holy Days now officially observed in Great Britain are Bank Holy Days; that the Athanasian Creed represents the best brief explication of the mysteries of the Financial Trinity, capital, currency, and credit; that the atmosphere and ritual of the bank is with difficulty distinguishable from that of the temple (in which, indeed, banking had its origin); and that the utterances of High Bankers and High Financiers have long had that note of lofty, solemn obscurantism that has marked the utterances of High Priests in all ages of religious petrifaction. And it is interesting, and I think significant, that the present tragic drama of the superstitious adoration of the gold totem has all been played before, ages ago, when the Ark of the Covenant was cherished so fanatically by the Israelites; when it was paraded before, and captured by, the hostile Philistines to whom it brought such desolation and woe that in the end they begged and bribed the late enemy to come and fetch it away.

The faith which should breathe in the soul

of Finance declines to a degraded superstition. High Priest becomes High Wizard. We are back among tribal superstitions and tribal rites. The High-Priest-Wizard, concerned no longer with faith, conducts a ritual about a totem. For a time he will slacken his insistence on our ceremonial adorations, allowing an easy-going and even exuberant manner of life to the tribe; then seized by some superstitious love or terror of the totem, he imposes the ritual with penitent severity. That is where we are now, or where we were until nine weeks ago.

Industry has work to do, and wants to do it. For these many years past it has been baffled and spell-bound by forces not its own. This thing cannot go on. Either Finance reforms its church, or industry, and with industry industrial civilisation, turns to Moscow or to the desert. Take the curse from industry, and industry will give the world good service. The conditions of employment will require constant adjustment, friction will arise, interruptions will occur. There are questions of industrial relations. The relations of employers and workpeople are also in part a matter of machinery, in greater part a matter of spirit. In the development of better machinery for the avoidance of disputes and a better spirit in the conduct of industrial relations the foundation of the Montague Burton Chair of Industrial Relations will, I hope and believe, be an influence for good.